How To Build Your Credit And Grow Financially

By: Arolfo Delacruz

PREFACE

© Copyright 2018 by Arolfo Delacruz- All rights reserved.

This document is geared towards providing exact and reliable information in regards to the topic and issue covered. The publication is sold with the idea that the publisher is not required to render accounting, officially permitted, or otherwise, qualified services. If advice is necessary, legal or professional, a practiced individual in the profession should be ordered.

From a Declaration of Principles which was accepted and approved equally by a Committee of the American Bar Association and a Committee of Publishers and Associations.

In no way is it legal to reproduce, duplicate, or transmit any part of this document in either electronic means or in printed format. Recording of this publication is strictly prohibited and any storage of this document is not allowed unless with written permission from the publisher. All rights reserved.

The information provided herein is stated to be truthful and consistent, in that any liability, in terms of inattention or otherwise, by any usage or abuse of any policies, processes, or directions contained within is the solitary and utter responsibility of the recipient reader. Under no circumstances will any legal responsibility or blame be held against the publisher for any reparation, damages, or monetary loss due to the information herein, either directly or indirectly.

Respective authors own all copyrights not held by the publisher.

The information herein is offered for informational purposes solely, and is universal as so. The presentation of the information is without contract or any type of guarantee assurance.

The trademarks that are used are without any consent, and the publication of the trademark is without permission or backing by the trademark owner. All trademarks and brands within this book are for clarifying purposes only and are the owned by the owners themselves, not affiliated with this document.

TABLE OF CONTENTS

REBUILD CREDIT HISTORY
Creation Of Credit

Effect Of Bad Credit

Good Credit

Requesting A Secure Card

About Credit Companies

What You Can Do

Choosing Your Investments

BUILD YOUR CREDIT
What Credit Score Is

Getting A Credit Rating You Can Be Proud Of Fast

THINGS TO AVOID
Were Your Spending Habits Out Of Control?

Did You Spend On Your Credit Card Without Thought?

Did You Have An Emergency That Was Not Catered For?

How Can Credit Change Your Life

How Is My Credit Score Calculated?

How Can I Check my Credit Score?

The Credit Card Secret

FINAL REMARKS

INTRODUCTION

Thank you for downloading this amazing guide—" **How To Build Your Credit And Grow Financially.**"

Credit is something we all need to survive in this world, and how you handle your credit will dictate how well your peers, employers, and moneylenders will be willing to do business with you. A good credit score means that you handle your finances responsibly and that you can be trusted with other people's money.

Are you looking for a way to begin to get closer to high or even perfect credit? Do you currently have bad or no credit and you are becoming sick of being turned down for loans, jobs, and other things because of your credit? There are many ways to go about building your credit, and the first step is to understand how it works.

First, if you have bad credit, then you have taken about 10 steps back from having no credit. If you have had some loans that you have not paid on time, defaulted on, or have been taken to court over, then you should know that it is a long road ahead, but you can still get to a much better place with your credit. You will need guidance to get there and i will help you by explaining the important steps.

REBUILD CREDIT HISTORY

Managing your daily life around your income is very important. The amount of spending and transactions is what drives the economy. Credit is money you don't have and is why it has a significant impact on the economy. Most people believe cash is worth more than credit, but they both hold the same value in spending. This is one tool the rich use to become wealthy. It is imperative to have a good credit score to gain trust from anybody in business, especially if you have little to no cash to back you up.

The bank will not give you a loan without proper credit or some cash. The secret is that you can open your own business with just credit by learning and gaining enough information to get a head start and outsmarting the bank. The bank controls the amount of credit they give you but remember they need you for business and allowing them to gain control of you will get you into debt. Using multiple skills will teach you to triple your income. Many investors flip credit, they also manage million dollar companies that developed with credit.

Creation Of Credit

Credit is created when you borrow money and agree to pay it later. When you open a credit line, it becomes an asset to the bank with the percentage in interest they charge. Credit is considered "debt" once you owe it back to the bank. Credit becomes an asset to you if you use it correctly or for investments. When you make a yearly salary of 40,000 and have a credit line of 10,000, you have access to 50,000. Credit is essential in the short run as well as the long term.

Certain people become wealthy using their own money. Most people become wealthy using other people money. For example, John has no money in the bank and is living check to check.

John currently has no debt and has a good credit history. The bank trust John and they are willing to increase his credit limit (Usually this is done by asking your bank). It is the bank business, and they will try to get that high interest paid. John now has a high enough credit limit to start his online store.

He will use the bank money (credit) to start it and then using the customer's money to pay the bank back. Remember, the bank would hate to see you go as a customer and they can do a lot of negotiating to keep you with them.

According to www.investopedia.com, Credit investing is what Credit market refers to the market through which companies and governments issue debt to investors, such as investment-grade bonds, junk bonds, and short-term commercial paper. I highly recommend you to self-teach yourself to maintain a low-interest rate.

What is the interest rate: Example- If you borrow money and the interest rate is 4% a year, it will cost you 4% of the amount borrowed. It will need to be paid along with the original money you borrowed. Interest rates are usually quoted annually but not always, so make sure you check. The higher your credit scores, the lower the interest rate?

There are times when the interest rates are meager in general. It usually happens when the economy is not good. When rates were first cut to their current levels in 2008-2009, it looked like a temporary expedient; now it looks like normality. The last time rates were low was around 2013.

They call it the economy wave when interest rates go up and down depending on the economy. According to MyFico.com mortgage rates vary by different credit score ranges.

The national average annual percentage rate, or APR, on a 30-year fixed-rate mortgage for a person with a FICO score between 760 and 850 is 3.77%. For a person with a credit score between 620 and 639, the national average APR is 5.36%. The difference in interest rates shows why it's so important to get your credit history on track before applying for a loan.

CATEGORY	SCORE
Excellent (30% of People)	750 - 850
Good (13% of People)	700 - 749
Fair (18% of People)	650 - 699
Poor (34% of People)	550 - 649
BAD (16% of People)	350 - 549

Effect Of Bad Credit

Having bad credit affects you in many ways. Credit affects your insurance premiums. It includes auto, life, and home insurance.

A bad credit history means you'll pay more for insurance than you would if you had better credit. Bad credit can stop you from being approved to get credit cards and all another type of loans which means you would have to pay cash for everything. There are times when we don't have the cash to buy essential things and even if we have just enough it's better to save it for later.

State and city jobs check credit at times and not having good credit can have you missing out on opportunities. Buying a new car, renting out an apartment, purchasing a new house and living stress-free are options you would like to have. Building your credit score and allowing the bank to trust you is the way to go. According to www.thebalance.com (LaToya Irby published May 09,

2017) Society is becoming increasingly dependent on using credit to make purchases and decisions.

Good Credit

These days, good credit is used for more than just getting a credit card or a loan. More and more businesses are making the case that you must have good credit before they extend products or services to you. It Affects Where You Live, and How Much You Pay Before you can buy a house, mortgage lenders want to know that you won't default on your mortgage. If you don't have good credit, the lender will consider it risky to give you a mortgage loan.

If you're approved for a mortgage, your credit affects your interest rate which directly impacts your monthly mortgage payment. Bad credit could mean a higher mortgage payment.

Worse than that, your mortgage application could be turned down because of your bad credit. Don't think that because you're not looking to buy a house right now that your credit isn't necessary. Landlords also use your credit to decide whether to rent to you.

Landlords consider your lease as a loan. You're being loaned a place to live, and the landlord wants to know you'll pay back this loan. If you don't have good credit, you can get denied for an apartment. Good credit gives you more options to make more significant decisions in life.

Tons of money is not needed to build your credit score while continuing your daily life. Imagine the economy with no credit. It would force everybody to work harder due to the amount of spending we do. An economy with credit allows us to take out loans and make transactions which are what drives the economy. As for credit cards, the trick is how to use it, the timing you have until interest hits, and how good you plan.

The loan is money we do not have, and this is what increases your yearly spending.

THIS IS ALSO WHAT CAN INCREASE YOUR YEARLY INCOME. The amount of credit in the United States is approximately 55 trillion dollars, and the amount of cash is only 4 trillion. It is too easy for the central bank to print out money as our spending will grow, and the total amount of interest will decrease.

The bank is too smart to do that because with no interest it will slow them down. The central banks are all competing with each other. Educating yourself and using this method you can have them give you what you need. A good quote Warren Buffet used, *"Risk comes from not knowing what you're doing."*

Reading and comparing facts are important before even applying to anything. Educating yourself is one of the essential techniques as I mention a lot within this section.

Understand what you are getting into and know what current interest rate you currently have. Credit score building is the easy stuff. The building process cost you nothing. When beginning to start your credit line, gaining some history is always a good start.

Requesting A Secure Card

Requiring a secure card is an excellent way to build your credit. A secure card is when you add your own money to a particular card and use it as a credit card. Credit builders are also very helpful and should be asked about; many banks offer this system to new customers. The bank allows you to open a secured card with a minimum of 100 - 250 depending on which bank you have. The bank then will use that amount as your "limit." Use the card and pay it monthly as if it was a regular credit card.

The bank will keep a record on how you use the card. When you are ready to move on you can withdraw the amount in the secure card. It is always good to check your credit score every month and see where you at. Call the bank and do not be afraid to ask "how much history do they have on file." It will give you an idea of how much longer until you request another actual credit card within the same year.

Checking your credit score can be done by free apps and websites like credit karma or credit sesame. Suppose you have a bad credit score and have a history. This technique will work perfectly fine to rebuild. Make sure your payments are on time, and you have less than 5 hard inquiries if more no problem. All credit report has approximately 10%-20% of errors on them. According to the Federal Trade

Commission, 20% of consumers who dispute credit report errors see their scores rise as a result. If you have college loans, this credit inquiry will hurt your credit score badly if you do not pay them on time. Call them and negotiate with them if you cannot pay them on time or are currently unemployed, DO NOT forget about them and let them keep charging the payments because they love charging high interest. They are always willing to negotiate, it all depends on how you speak and what you can offer.

When using your secure card, only use 10-30 percent of the total amount. Try your best to pay it in full by the due date. It will increase your credit score and better your history. Always remember it is important only to have 2 inquiries every 18 months. The bank records every 24 months, but 18 will not hurt you.

About Credit Companies

Beware of the credit companies that charge you money to fix your credit. (The things they do you can do them yourself). Students can start building the credit as well.

According to Mike Sullivan, former director of education for taking Charge America, a Phoenix-based nonprofit financial education and consumer debt service organization. He recommends parents when the student is going off to college, unless you're 100 percent sure they're responsible, the first credit card that student should have is yours.

What You Can Do
I used this technique myself, and I was not in college at the time. I used it to gain my parent's credit history. When you go under someone else credit you increase the history they already have. I recommend you to check before you go under anybody credit because going on someone credit with bad credit makes no sense.

This is what I call a "credit booster." Using a secure card and gaining someone else credit history can get you where you need to be quick. Having an income helps but is not necessary to start building, all you need is enough to get the secure card. When you hit 650-750, you see improvements in your credit score.

Once you notice the change and is near the 700s, you can start looking for a credit limit increase. Some credit cards will increase it themselves within the first few months of "on time" payments and low usage. Depending on timing your credit line should be around 5,000- 10,000 if you followed the steps. You have control of your credit score and this is considered a good credit score, 750 and above is excellent. Maintenance is what is called from now on.

Eliminating old credit inquiries and maintaining 100% credit payments. You can open different credit cards and use the ones returning right amount of points. Credit card reward points are excellent when you apply them to your goal.

For example, chase sapphire preferred offers a good chunk of points if you use a certain amount within 3 months that can be transferred to a free hotel room, free flights, cash, etc. Combining 2 good credit cards can pay for themselves. This is next level, no more baby steps. Communication can get you far, as we all learn while growing up.

Think of it as if you were in trouble with your parents and you are finding any excuse to get out of being punished. Now is a great time to use it to get what you need. I paid one of my credit cards recently and felt like the interest was too high to continue to use it.

I called the bank and explained to that I needed another year with no interest because I felt like it was too high. They did transfer me to a few customer service representatives and questioned me a few times, but in the end, I got what I want. I was able to use the credit card for one more year with no interest.

When upgrading to better credit cards with better reward points, yearly fees may apply.

Usually, you get one free year with no interest and no annual fees. I recommend you to use any credit cards wisely if needed only. It is ok to take advantage for the one free year but if not required make the phone call and downgrade to one with no annual fees.

Investing is not all about starting significant and being a baller from the start, you need to begin with small amounts of money and increase the amount as you get comfortable with the process. It may be deciding not to go to a fast food restaurant or passing on the night out with friends and saving the money instead. Investing credit is not a get rich fast scheme or something that will make you rich.

You can't go and try to invest your loans into stock you have no information about. Becoming a successful investor takes time, effort, and a lot of discipline, but keeping in mind these four basic investing techniques should help every beginning investor get off to a great start.

Choosing Your Investments
Warren Buffett, a huge proponent of long-term investing and a wellspring of financial wisdom, advises that you should "only buy something that you'd be perfectly happy to hold if the market shut down for 10 years." Choose your investments based on solid fundamentals and strong long-term prospects, not because you think a stock's price is poised to rise only in the short-run.

Markets and individual stock prices fluctuate over time, but keep your eye on the long-term, and invest in high-quality companies with consistent performance and experienced management teams. When you buy a property with a mortgage, each month your loan balance decreases.

It means, over time, your tenant is essentially paying the loan down for you, helping you build wealth automatically. To make this concept clearer, pretend for a moment you owned a property that you bought for

$1,000,000 with a mortgage of $800,000, and it earned $0 in cash flow (it "broke even") and never climbed in value.

However, after that thirty-year mortgage is paid off, you'll now have a property worth $1,000,000 that you didn't save for. Your tenant paid it off due to the "loan pay-down."

Proofing your yearly income if you have a job and at least 2 years of working at the same job can get you a mortgage loan. It is essential to know if you want to get into real estate investing.

Real estate investments are significant. Passive income is when you can be home sleeping and still make money. Real estate, buying stocks and an ecommerce business are all examples of passive income. Enjoy the process and live free while doing it. It's all about being wealthy and happy at the end of the day.

BUILD YOUR CREDIT

A solid credit score can lead to lower interest rates, loan approvals, and even job opportunities. If your score is currently less than what you would like it to be, you can take measures to improve it. By understanding the basics of the system, you can start building your credit score today.

What Credit Score Is

The term "credit score" refers to the overall health of your finances. The Fair Isaac Corporation usually calculates this three-digit figure. Fair Isaac takes information from your credit report and punches the numbers through a series of calculations.

Your payment history and the amount of outstanding debt you have been taken into consideration. The length of credit, new credit, and type of credit you have are also reviewed.

Before issuing credit, many lenders check your credit score. You may be accepted or denied based on your credit score. For this reason, it is essential to maintain a good score. And doing so can be easy. Following are some steps you can take to help you build your credit score.

- **Make Payments on Time**

By far the easiest and best way to build your credit score is to avoid late payments. By paying bills on time, you show lenders that you are reliable and consistent. If you have a hard time remembering when payments need to be made, try streamlining the due dates.

Call your lenders and ask to have the due date changed to a particular day of the month. Set up all your bills to be due on the same date. You can also line up automatic payments. That way, the money is withdrawn from your checking account at the same time each month. Have reminders sent to your email or mailbox? Find a method that helps you pay on time, every time.

- **Pay Down Your Debt**

Paying off debts that you have is another way to build your credit score. Strive to use only 35% or less of your credit limit. So if you have two credit cards that each have a $5,000 limit, you have a total credit limit of $10,000. Aim to keep your total outstanding balances under $3,500. It will lower your credit risk, thereby raising your credit score.

- **Keep Accounts Open**

If you have had a credit card for a long time and rarely use it, think twice before closing the account. If you have a solid history of on-time payments, it may be in your best interest to keep the account open. It will show lenders that you have a longer credit history.

- **Use your Credit Card Wisely**

Building your credit score does not mean getting rid of your credit cards or not using them. But before you make a purchase, consider how you will pay it back. Look into what you can and cannot afford before swiping the plastic.

If you decide to open a new account, keep your shopping time limited to 14 days. Once you have the credit card, pay off your balances on a timely basis. It will improve your credit score over time.

Getting A Credit Rating You Can Be Proud Of Fast

When it comes to your credit, you have to understand how important it is. Having good credit does not mean that you can get a loan whenever you want. It says much more than just getting the financing you want when it is time to get it.

If you want to build your credit, you have to know what it is going to take to do so and that requires that you understand what all goes into your credit report. Here are some things you need to consider before you start building credit for yourself.

1. What can credit do for you?

Credit is a significant thing in our society, and it can do many things for you if you have good credit.

Some employers use a credit check as part of their screening process for hiring new employees, and if you have bad credit, it could be the deciding factor in whether or not you get a job.

Credit can also determine whether you pay a more substantial amount of money for car insurance, home insurance, and life insurance. Plus, of course, credit is a deciding factor in all financial transactions like loans, getting a cell phone, or anything else that requires good credit.

2. How can you make sure you always have good credit?

When it comes to having good credit, there are some things you need to understand to build your credit. You have to understand that you do lose points on your credit score for having too many companies look into your credit in a 90 day period.

It means that when you shop for a loan or something else that is going to require credit you need to be very careful about who you let pull your credit and how many times you allow it to happen.

Also, if you want to build your credit, you need to understand that paying your bills on time is essential, but making sure your credit cards are paid in full or very close to it is even more critical.

3. What to do next?

The last thing that has to be discussed is how you are going to get a better credit rating. The best way to start is to get a copy of your credit report and start looking at all the debts you have that are on the delinquent side of the report.

It means that you were late on at least one payment with these debts. Start with the smallest debts you have and pay them off, and then work up towards the more substantial debts over time. By paying off anything on the delinquent side of the report, you will be building better credit almost immediately, and this will help you with anything that involves credit.

THINGS TO AVOID

If your credit has been damaged, it is time to vow to yourself to never get back into the same situation and to now work on repairing your credit. When trying to build your credit, you need to recognize what sent you on the path to a bad credit report in the first place and work to avoid these things in the future.

Were Your Spending Habits Out Of Control?

Set up a budget so that you can learn to control your spending. A budget will help you to recognize what expenses you must cover and what expenses are uncontrolled spending. Know what is coming in and what goes out: certain expenses must be covered, and you will see how much you have left for payment towards debt and sundry expenses.

Think before you buy. Do you need that new outfit or are you spending to keep up with fashion and feed your desire for new things? Save for purchases rather than using the credit card.

If you find yourself in a situation where you might not be able to get out of debt on your own, there are credit counseling centers that can help you repair your credit. Not only can they help repair your credit, but they can also help you make a plan to avoid getting into credit trouble again.

Did You Spend On Your Credit Card Without Thought?

The best thing you can do for yourself when you are trying to repair your credit is to get rid of your credit card debt and then stop using the card. Use it sparingly.

In your budget, you will allow for certain spendings such as for clothing and gifts. Make sure you have allowed enough for these each year and stuck to your limits. Avoid using the credit card for these purchases. Pay your balance on time. Never miss a payment. It is always best to repay in full each month and avoid interest charges but at the very least repay more than the minimum required.

Put your cards in place you can't quickly get to or ask a trusted friend to keep them for you.

If your credit card debt is too much for you to manage on your own, contact a debt consolidation company and apply for a debt consolidation loan that will pay off all of your creditors and allow you to make just one payment instead of several.

Did You Have An Emergency That Was Not Catered For?

Having an emergency that requires unanticipated spending on credit cards can send you into debt.

Once you have got your debts under control start an emergency fund to avoid, this happening to you again. Aim for two to three months' worth of income.

If your credit if it is less than perfect take positive steps now to rebuild your credit. You will find that it will be well worth the time and effort to know that you are considered creditworthy and to have your debts under control.

How Can Credit Change Your Life

Everybody knows that bad credit is not one of life's pleasures, and dealing with credit debt is one of the hardest things a person has to face during their lives. But we don't mention why it is essential to get out of bad credit. No, it is not only to make those figures look nicer on our credit report, or buy a more expensive car. The main reason is that bad credit steals your life!

A person who is trying to get out of bad credit has to face loads of challenges. First of all: they have to face the situation rationally, and that is the worst part. Not lying about the position, but assessing our credit debt and trying to find a solution.

It can be a great shock for many people, especially when we are talking about massive credit card debt that only started with a couple of hundred pounds, and not being aware of the speed the interest increased the amount now we cannot even pay the minimum payment.

But other than the shock people get when facing their real financial situation, there are loads of other things bad credit can affect lives. We are going to go through a couple of aspects and trying to give you advice on how to deal with every one.

- **Bad credit affects your job**

You might not be able to concentrate on your job at the workplace if your head is full of problems and worries. You are going to miss the next opportunity for promotion, or if it gets even worse, you might lose your job, making your financial situation even worse.

Or if you were planning a career change, you might have to postpone it because without a job you will never get a chance to get out of the bad credit situation you are in. Staying in a job you hate will cause even more stress and frustration, making it harder to deal with credit debt. My advice is to keep level-headed at work and try not to show your frustration. Leave your problems outside the entrance, and pick them up when you finished.

- **Bad credit affects your relationship**

It is a well-known fact that financial issues are the leading causes of divorce. Stress leads to loads of misunderstanding. Therefore we don't want to communicate or blame each other for their credit situation.

Nobody wants to admit that they caused the problem, or they could have been more careful, and take on the "attack-defense" strategy that will never help to find a solution.

Try to take joint responsibility for your finances, and work together on the answers. It helps if you do a financial assessment together, brainstorm about ideas, and try to focus on the future and not the past.

☐ **Bad Credit affects your health**

Like every situation, you feel that your hands are tied, and you are going round and round, dealing with credit problems will cause you an enormous amount of stress.

And scientists have long ago discovered that stress causes many symptoms that will eventually lead to mental or physical illness. Stress also causes abuse of substances that are making your financial situation even worse. A couple of illnesses bad credit might cause are depression, hair loss, diabetes, heart disease, sexual dysfunction.

A Simple Number

A credit score is a numerical value that determines the risk factor of a borrower and is the main reason why people have trouble arranging a loan.

The higher your credit scores are, the better. A high credit score is deemed 615-650+ while a lower credit score is 500 or below.

How Is My Credit Score Calculated?

Credit bureaus use their mathematical algorithm to determine an individual's credit score and therefore risk factor.

The credit bureau's keep this algorithm a secret in fear of credit score manipulation and the possibility of someone using the information to harm.

However, it isn't all bad news. What we don't know is what percentage of factors are taken into account.

Do they penalize you 20% or 30% if you have had a bankruptcy? 5% or 10% if you have a had a judgment against you?

That is their little secret. However what we do know are the causes that tend to move credit score values.

CREDIT SCORE FACTORS

- Bankruptcy
- Judgments
- Tax arrears
- Consumer proposal
- Late payments (3 months or more)
- Debt in collections (Listed as "R9" on credit bureau)
- Living off of credit (Always applying for more)
- Credit bureau inquiries (too many companies looking at your credit bureau)

- ☐ Late payments (1-2 months not as big a deal as 3+)

All of the reasons above are very influential in affecting a credit rating.

Some manage to do more credit damage than others, like a bankruptcy. While others such as credit inquiries are not as severe.

How Can I Check my Credit Score?

The first step to checking your credit rating is to request a copy of your credit bureau. You can request a copy through the major bureau Equifax or request it through your lender.

Borrowers are allowed one copy a year for their curiosity and to check for errors that may hinder their score. When creditors report on your credit bureau, it is assumed that their information is correct and in most cases everything is factual.

However, in some cases, there are errors in the reporting that can do severe damage to a consumer's credit bureau that will go unnoticed. Although not your fault, the responsibility now lies on you to catch these mistakes if they do happen.

Your credit is worth being paid attention to, and everyone should be concerned about their score and how to improve it. Financial institutions use it to profile you and assess your character and pay top dollar to their employees to break down your file and determine if you are trustworthy.

Had a bankruptcy? You can't budget. Debt that is in collections? You are a deadbeat. These are the things they say, and although may not be true, they couldn't care less. Motivate yourself not to be labeled and held back by being responsible with your finances.

The Credit Card Secret

It is possible to obtain property with no money down using readily accessible zero interest credit cards.

If you are looking to purchase low-cost properties, then this can be done by using credit cards. To do this, you only apply for a credit card who issues associated cheques.

Remember that anything and everything in life is negotiable. That means that if you think that that the credit limits on your card is low, you can ask your bank to increase it. The thing to remember here is that they want YOUR business and they are a lot of hanks competing for it, so they will probably be more than happy to do this for you.

You can then use these credit cards to pay for the deposit and then get a mortgage for the rest, or if your balance is high enough, the entire property.

The next step is then to apply for another credit card and then take advantage of their "introductory balance transfer rate" where you pay zero percent for around 6 months.

After about 5 months, you then apply for a third credit card offering this introductory rate.

It seems madness, but this is a straightforward thing to do, and it does work!. Many investors used this idea to make their first property purchase.

FINAL REMARKS

Once you have built your credit profile to the point that you can obtain unsecured loans by yourself, it is vital to continue to build and protect it. It is easy to destroy your credit, and it can happen extremely fast, but repairing your credit can be difficult and very time-consuming.

Maintaining your credit is an endless job, but it is a lot easier to do the steps to manage it than it is to repair it. Having good credit is essential to having the good things in life that you will want.

So whether you're reestablishing your credit after a financial crisis, or struggling to establish your credit for the very first time, you can use these simple steps to get your foot in the door of the credit world.

Keep in mind that a good credit history will only bring you benefits.

Motivational Quote

"Success is not final; failure is not fatal: It is the courage to continue that counts."

-- Winston S. Churchill

www.ingramcontent.com/pod-product-compliance
Lightning Source LLC
Chambersburg PA
CBHW031559210526
45464CB00003B/1353